Dog on Oils

TRACEY L. SCHREIBER

Change your mind. Change your dog.

Dog On Oils

Copyright © 2019 Tracey L. Schreiber

All Rights Reserved. Published in association with Whole Life Press a division of SpeakTruth Media Group, LLC, www.speaktruthmedia.com.

Author's Disclaimer: The information contained in this book is for educational purposes only. I'm not a licensed professional, just simply sharing what I have learned and applied, along with the results I've seen in my own pets and that of other pet owners I have worked with to change dog behaviors. Every dog is different, it takes time, patience, love, and follow through to see lasting results. For aggressive dogs, consult a professional to help bring balance and control to your pet. I am here to help. Reach out to me at www.dogonoils.com.

Book art design, layout, and cover design by Leslie Kinney for SpeakTruth Media Group in collaboration with Tracey L. Schreiber.

Photography Credit: Leslie Kinney

Stock Photo Credit: Golden Retriever ©Eric Isselee/123RF.com

ISBN 978-1-7342646-0-9 (pbk)

First Edition: December 2019

Printed in the United States of America

Dedication

To my husband, my hero, Ron, for always safely trusting and believing in me. Thanks for loving me enough to say, "Yes!" to the adventure.

Table of Contents

Love Letter To A Dog...A *Ruff* Start! 2

We Don't Need No *Stinkin'* Oils 8

The Navy Seals Who *Rearranged* My Brain 16

Keep Calm, And *Carry-On*...Like A Porcupine! 26

The *Barkers* Dozen 34

A Life With No *Pulling* 40

Puppy *Nose* Best 46

Tips and Tricks to Help You *Pass* The Storm Drain 54

Essential Oils You Need NOW and Why 61

About the Author 67

Praise for Tracey the Transformation Junkie 69

Dog On Oils

Chapter One
Love Letter To A Dog...
A *Ruff* Start!

1

Jesus painted such a beautiful and significant picture of a real, authentic relationship when He said, *"There is no greater love than a man lay down his life for his friend."* Through those words, I see Christ laying down His *royal heritage*, dying for us because of His great love for all people.

My experience with dogs throughout my life paints the same image. They *are* man's best friend on this earth. Now, I've learned what we can give them in return. We can lay down our stress, anger, hate, and anxiety for their benefit. Friend, those benefits are many, and you are going to learn about them right here in the pages of this book.

As we choose to let go of the things that hurt us, and ultimately them, we are set free from bondage and illness as a beautiful side effect to this marvelous exchange of love. Dogs, like God, love unconditionally and give us an outlet of God's healing as we let go of the things that cause us pain. I know the release of this love exchange well because I have received so much over the years through my friendship with dogs.

As a child, I spent the Summer with my dad each

year, and his neighborhood was filled with dogs roaming around. During a time when I had numerous unseen challenges, I found great comfort and confidence through dogs. I spent time teaching those pups how to sit, stay, lay down, and so on. As they learned and responded with joy, it left me feeling empowered and quite frankly like the boss of something.

In my own small, but right way, I was taking dominion over the dogs I interacted with on those hot summery days. Through those experiences, I learned about taking authority as a youngster. As a grown-up, I've learned to apply that knowledge inwardly and take dominion over my own body to positively affect my health, my family, my community, and, most notably, my pack of dogs.

Over those years of receiving comfort from many pups, I recognized how their love helped me. They gave me moments of joy, and their love was like a prayer interceding for my pain to give me hope. In many ways, they changed my thinking. And here's the take-away. When you change your thinking, everything changes, even your dog, which is why I wrote this book. I want to teach you the mechanics of thought and emoting around your pet.

So, to the title of this book, *Dog On Oils*, the most beautiful thing second to the companionship and loyalty of a dog is the fact that every dog is a diffuser, and I love to diffuse essential oils *everywhere*! Most of the time, dogs gleefully diffuse slobber and pure love, but when you add essential oil to their coat to help their behavior, emotions, or to soothe an infirmity, they, in turn, diffuse the aroma releasing significant wellness benefits both for them and us. It's a win-win! Hence the title, Dog On Oils! Get it?

Trust me, your dog needs oils, wants oils, and will be happy, happy, happy to get oils.

When I first realized I needed a dog, I didn't recognize how much a dog needed me. But, God's love is so profoundly seen through them; they are a perfect match for joy in this life. So here's to God's gift of dogs and my love letter to every single one of them that has and will cross my path. May I be better for having them and them for having me.

> **Trust me, your dog needs oils, wants oils, and will be happy, happy, happy to get oils.**

Oh, the lessons in love you taught me.
When I had no confidence, you patiently
stood by my side.
When I sat and cried, you rested your head
next to mine.
When the storms of life came through, I
looked around, and there was you.
You would, without a second thought,
lay down your life for mine,
Just like the greatest Love Story of all time.
You dance around when I dance around
and wait for me at the door.
I will always work to be the companion to

*you that you are to me,
I'm just afraid this side of heaven
I will always fall short.
But, I promise to do my best to give you
exactly what you need.
Thank you for your love unconditional,
for in this world, it's a beauty to find. Learning
always from you, but mostly, you've taught
me the meaning of KIND. And, for that, I'm
eternally grateful for you.*

The more pet parents understand, the better people we become. So let's learn how to achieve a beautiful and balanced life together. NOW — without further ado, join me on a journey to freedom as we learn about behavior, science, and God's garden gifts for our pet's wellness.

Dog On Oils

Chapter Two
We Don't Need No Stinkin' Oils

2

LOL! Or, so I thought!

We don't need no stinking oils! Yeah, I said it all the time with my sassy self. It makes me laugh every time I think of it or say it. But how does it apply to a dog on oil? Well, I'm about to tell you!

I've been an advocate and fan of Young Living Essential Oils for close to thirteen years, off and on, and avidly for the past four. I believe in the company's quality because of their Seed to Seal® promise, guaranty of purity, and founder, Gary Young's *"never let go like a bulldog"* tenacity for results. I've had the pleasure to teach on the oils and be a part of certification classes that equip users with greater knowledge and understanding. Without a doubt, I would use an essential oil over a pharmaceutical any day, unless there's an emergency requiring immediate attention. No popping pills for me! I'm always diffusing essential oils because of the benefits to my wellness, and because I want to walk in full health. I do this to support and balance my body in the best way.

When it comes to a dog's behavior, emotions, attitude, and physical energy, essential oils make a big difference in their stability. And, essential oils are proven to have a significant effect on emotions, anxiety, and the overall energy we exude. For example, a person's fear translates to a dog, causing the dog to react with negative behaviors. You don't necessarily need an essential oil to help your dog, but if you have them, like me (Lord knows this girl is rarely without a purse full of essential oils!), you can use them to change the atmosphere around you. Essential oils are a tool you can use for a myriad of issues, but using them to calm yourself and your dog is a biggie.

In situations where you are without essential oils or any tool for that matter, you can still be empowered! And, I am about to empower you with the knowledge you need to take charge of your life and your dog's. Are you excited? I am!

When I recognize that a dog needs to burn off some energy through activities like running, I often envision myself on a skateboard letting that dog pull me like a sled. Thank goodness, my oldest son Ron talked me out of attempting this sport on several occasions. Here's the deal, skateboards, bikes, rollerblades, and scooters can give you a unique advantage for helping high energy dogs fulfill their activity needs. Like a treadmill or even a pronged collar, yikes, can enable better communication with your dog. In many cases you are giving direction to all their energy. By the way, I'm a massive fan the pronged collar when using the right approach, not for correction but instruction. These collars can bring POSITIVE progress with your dog. But I digress! The bottom line to burning off energy is that you can change everything about your dog. Your mindset, even your thinking can help your dog calm down, which lowers their energy. When you combine positive thinking and exercise with essential oils, you have a powerhouse of tools to help your dog live a full and happy life.

I've also learned that releasing my emotions is a crucial factor for optimal health, and it helps keep my animals balanced and well, too, which produces a glorious side effect. Our emotions cause us to think. What thoughts are filling your mind right now? Really? Think about it! If your thoughts are bringing negative emotions, you need to let those go. There are a couple of essential oil blends that can help you release those thought patterns like Peace & Calming® or Present Time™. When I recognize I am worrying about something I want those thoughts and feelings out of my brain as quickly as possible. Even Frankincense has a chemical constituent that helps you focus on one thing at a time. Your state of mind affects your dog's state of mind, so being calm helps the dog be calm and gives him a more significant ability to be directed in the way you want him to behave.

I have been regularly training a sweet pup named Tucker for some time. He's an awesome dog, but young

> If your thoughts are bringing negative emotions, you need to let those go.

with a lot of energy. I've noticed that he has a gift to help with evaluating other dogs. He also seems to be tuned in to what is going on in our minds. When Tucker's mama tells me about his behaviors, we realize he is being affected by what she is thinking. Understanding that the dog is picking up on your thinking and reacting to it will help you bring peace and calm to your dog. When your dog is misbehaving, pay attention to your thoughts and adjust if necessary. Mindfulness is required. I say, *"Mindfulness to the max!"* And speaking of Max! He is another one of my regular trainees. I tell his mama that he is brought quickly to *"balance,"* in large part because I believe he will come into balance, so he *is*. Are you making the connection? Again, your thinking affects the dog's behavior.

In the case of all the overly energetic little dogs that like to lay down or not move forward on a walk, when I walk them, they will always get up quickly and go, that is, *if* they lay down at all. Bently and Emmy come to mind and countless others. While their mamas think, "Oh my baby with his *little* legs cannot walk that far," I am having this conversation in my head, "You are young, full of *energy*, and I saw you leap to the top of the couch in a single bound." I know that little dog can make the walk with no problem. So, I expect it beforehand. It's all about expectations. Like when dealing with my grandchildren, whether it's the car seat, diapering, or riding in the grocery cart, I imagine compliance, and most of the time, it works! It's all about how YOU see the situation. Kids and pets! Who knew? Never let them see you sweat.

When I work on a dog's behavior, at times, I give him what's called a *doggy raindrop,* based on a technique of feathering essential oils onto the spine and bottoms of the feet for humans. Using a modification of the method on a dog can be extremely beneficial. It boosts the immune system, detoxes the body, and is downright enjoyable for both dogs and people.

When I'm training a dog, and he becomes consistent with good behavior, I like to give him a Raindrop. I want the unique combination of oils and scents to be a marked smell that reminds the owner, dog, and myself of the time that their dog behaved admirably, which establishes a good association. The aroma brings us back to a specific place and time, like a dog training technique using a clicker to mark the experience for easy recall. Essential oils do the same thing marking the smells to relive the joyful occasion.

Our brains are marvelous and miraculous! And so is our God who created it!

Essential oils work instantly with the limbic system in your brain through the sense of smell — the only one of the five senses, where we respond emotionally before logically. Aromas give us the ability to reverse overthinking, worry, and a multitude of negative emotions that can affect our pup.

So, while I have used my sassy comment, *"we don't need no stinkin' oils,"* to make a point. The hilarious part of it is just like so many helpful resources that give us incredible advantages in our *"journey to balance"* with our dogs, pure essential oils are an incredible tool that we need to keep in our little bag to help our pets.

In reality, you need some stinkin', awesome oils for yourself and your dog! And I can and will help you get the best essential oils on the planet, bar none!

Dog On Oils

Chapter Three
The Navy Seals Who Rearranged My Brain

3

Two people have been instrumental in my journey of learning as much as I could about how to help dogs cope with their emotions and all the crazy things that unfold around them. I like to refer to these two people as the *Navy Seals that Rearranged My Brain*. And man did they change the way I think about so many things, including the behavior of dogs.

Have you ever heard of Cesar Millan, *The Dog Whisperer*? He took me from an animal lover to a sold-out strategic, evaluating, analyzing, implementing animal behaviorist. Step-by-step, he taught me every bit of wisdom I needed to know to not only handle my *"pack"* but help others understand and manage their own. I guarantee you if you follow his methods, you will see positive results. And it's simple. You must communicate with your dog as a pack leader would. My take away from this is that you must become a *"mama dog"* handling your pup the same way she was created to respond and give discipline.

So, I have a pack of thirteen, don't ask, you would not even believe the daily feats I used to go through to take care of them all. Just making their dinner — you have no idea! Let's say in years past; it was a *madhouse*. People kept asking me, *"Have you ever seen the dog whisperer?"* Or they'd say, *"Tracey, come to my house and watch the dog whisperer with us."* I kept hearing his name over and over, like a knock at the door! I thought, *"Who is this, Cesar?"* Finally, I found out who this *dog whisperer* was, put to practice what I learned from him, and my *pack* was never the same!

I have to admit, my introduction was slow coming, but as I studied his methods, I was empowered to enforce peace where there was no peace. I was amazed at how he shifted a person's psychological and emotional state through their dog. No Ph.D. was necessary! I'm not sure if Cesar has even an honorary Ph.D., but if I had one to give him, I'd do so quickly!

No doubt, God used Cesar to teach me how to let go of the past to affect my dogs and, ultimately, my life. He changed my brain and, therefore, my thinking. Now my life's motto is —change your thinking, change your dog. Don't stop there, let's go for the gold, change your thinking, change *everything!* That is a powerful truth right there!

Do you know when your energy is good, even birds and squirrels and lizards will come close to you? To that thought, my best friend Beverly would probably say, *"I will pass on that lizard thing!"* LOL!

Did I mention Beverly is my BFF? And, she's Navy Seal number two, who taught me about the power of emotional release, animals and essential oils, and even more. She has a Ph.D. in common sense and wisdom. She's a people whisperer! She also has the *"remain calm and carry on"* thing down. I learned this very early in our friendship when my son talked my daughter into eating a Tallow Tree leaf while outside jumping on the trampoline. I was the *"freak-out"* queen for the first twenty years of motherhood. I wish I understood the nature of calm energy while I was raising my kids. Especially the day I called poison control while having a nervous breakdown. Beverly kept telling me in a calm voice, *"everything is going to be fine."* I thought nothing of the sort! But, in the end she was right. For years she has been my beautiful, smart, cool friend who I looked to for wisdom.

Now I want to be *your* Navy Seal! So, here are **ten things you need to know right now to help your dog.**

#1 Give Your Dog a Job — exercise and fulfillment are crucial to earning trust with your dog. Walks equate to leadership! They are like *love on a leash*. Positively challenge your dog with activities — the higher the level of energy required, the better. Your dog's behavior will give you a clue to what he needs, like what a dog is bred to do. Is he/she a hunter? A retriever? Maybe he wants to herd the kids or hide objects! You can use these activities to engage your pup and fulfill the innate desires he or she is born to do. You get the idea!

#2 Be a Mama Dog — communicate with calm, gentle, but firm rules, boundaries, and limits. A well-timed touch or noise to express what you want is vital to provide direction that leads to a well behaved and balanced dog. Giving correction keeps you out of the bribery game. You can change the cycle, but rewards combined with mama dog boundaries and limits make for a more balanced approach to displaying leadership in your dog's brain.

#3 Making Time for Follow Through — patience is your greatest asset while achieving the goals for your dog. Setting up scenarios that give you this patient advantage keeps you in the first place and gives your dog the time to accept the experiences you want to happen. Make sure you are always one step ahead in terms of leading them to what you want. One example I'll write more about later is entering the car with no issues; you first! Making sure you allow for extra time creates the opportunity to accomplish what you want without the stress and frustration of time constraints.

#4 Think About What You're Thinking About — if your dog is acting out, take a deep breath and a quick inventory of what is on your mind. Many behaviors are turned around with a change of thoughts. Your energy is everything to a dog. Dogs are bi-lingual; they first understand your energy, then your body language. Be intentional about thinking positively and taking a leadership stance. Write down your goals for you and your pup, then get to believing! Train your brain

> Dogs are bi-lingual: they first understand your energy, then your body language.

for the great things you want to see in a dog. Consistently doing this is both powerful and effective. Raise your expectations for seeing the best in your dog, I mean you may get laughs for making a doggie vision board, but no one will be laughing at you when your pup is the best dog ever!

#5 Remember, Food and Treats Are Affection and Energy — think about this, physical energy comes and goes. Food, treats, cuddles, and excitement are all energy-producing, so before you extend any of these to your dog ask yourself, *"Have I subtracted some of his or her energy today?"* I call this *"doing the math"* of balance. Examples for subtracting energy are working for food, adding backpacks to walks, even using part of their meal as a treat to reward them as you work with them on commands they know, then reward them with the rest of the meal in a peaceful, enjoyable state. These types of energy subtracting activities will all help to establish leadership for you in your dog's eyes.

#6 Get the Right Leash For You And Your Pet — in an on-leash world; this tool becomes the hotline from your brain to your dog's brain. The leash should give you confidence and the ability to communicate with your dog. Check out my leash suggestions at dogonoils.com.

#7 When Your Dog Sees Your Face, Let Him See A Smile — dogs have very short memories of what just happened, approximately one to three seconds. So when dealing with a doggy offense, if it's beyond those few seconds, calm down, clean it up, let it go, and smile. With dogs, it is all about the patterns. Showing them a pattern of joy is an excellent way to get them to return to your side consistently.

#8 Resist the Urge To Nurture Insecurity — understanding when and how to nurture can be a hard lesson if you are just being introduced to the world of dog behavior. Dogs are not the same as human babies, caressing insecurity, excitement, or imbalance will only encourage the continuation of unwanted behavior. You need to learn what a *"mama dog response"* would be to these behaviors. I've learned this over the years and applied it when necessary; as you can imagine, the results are mind-blowing. But hey, mama dogs know best, right? So here's what she would do.

Mama dogs begin communicating what is and isn't accepted right away. I know, I had a front-row seat to the mother of all mama dog responses one day at a dear friend's house. I was smitten with their five-week-old Corgi pups. Watching them, I saw big sister begin to chew on her brother's ear mercilessly. Before I could remove the ear from the mouth of the puppy, mama dog Hallie got off her queen-sized dog bed, lept into the puppy box, and headbutted big sis knocking her off little brother. Well isn't that amazing for all those that think correction is mean? I say if mama dog does it we should too. A physical touch — gentle, quick, and well-timed is precisely what some unwanted behavior requires.

Recently I had the fantastic opportunity to fly to upstate New York and drive back a ten-week-old puppy to Texas, so that little Rubble would not have to fly back under a seat on a plane. During that trip, I learned enough to fill this book about the pressure we feel when deciding what is best for puppies when it comes to petting or consoling. Often, we give a wrong response to our pups that nurtures their insecurity. And if we'd been on a plane, those incorrect responses would have been at an all-time high. When a puppy cries or whines you have no choice but to console for the environment of the plane. However, I was blessed with a different opportunity to learn on this trip. So off we went through 1,900 miles of time to *"mama dog respond"* to this sweet boy.

When I put him in the car, he immediately began jumping and mouthing and acting puppy crazy. But in no time, I had him in his travel bag, and we were on our way. When he whined, I just gave the bag a little tap and the famous Cesar, *"Cht!"* Afterward, Rubble calmed down and went to sleep. We drove and stopped to stretch, potty, and have our meals; and stayed in a hotel two nights. I accomplished so much training over those three days. By the end of our trip, Rubble was potty trained, leash trained, and sleeping through the night. I used Lavender essential oil at night and curled up next to his travel bag on the hotel bed.

At ten-weeks-old, Rubble did a stellar job. If I spent our time cuddling him to settle him down or caressing him when he whined, it would have been another story. Remember, mama dogs cannot hug, hold, or stroke. They lick, gently push, and sometimes growl or snap. Not with an intent to harm, but to redirect the pup and let him know his behavior is not good.

Our behavior is always teaching our pups something. One of our dogs, Brewster Bear, a reasonably common name, right? LOL! When we picked him up from his mama dog and littermates, he cried and fussed all the way home, and you guessed it, we petted and consoled him. Occasionally we dealt with Brewster's lip-licking and tail tucked behavior, which always started an uproar with one of our other dogs. Actions that are rare these days, since we address him instead of allowing the other dog to go after him. We finally learned. Thank you, God, and thank you, Cesar! All of this is to say if we had ignored or corrected the insecure behavior, we would not have had the countless opportunities to deal with Brewster's nervousness that brought on unnecessary attacks.

It doesn't feel right to do things like a mama dog, but again remember, a dog is not an infant. Dogs have a different psychology. When you start acting like a mama dog as you respond to your pet, you will see results, and their behavioral changes will make you a believer.

#9 Don't Imagine The Worst When Leaving Your Pup Behind — there are many tools to support your dog when he/she is home alone. But the number one treat you can give your dog when you leave is your happy unguilty attitude. Your dog does not understand why you feel guilty. He will only know something upset you. So, leave them the blanket, a million toys, and safe, brain challenging, healthy chews. Diffuse Lavender or Peace and Calming® nearby. Most importantly, let go of anxious feelings and leave your dog behind with calm, happy thoughts.

#10 Use All of The Natural Resources Available To You To Positively Affect Your Dog — the environment, inclines, barriers, and so on can give you a physical advantage and good energy that gives you the psychological edge. Also, effectively use essential oils for helping your dog and you with emotional, mental, and practical applications.

Now you can be a Navy Seal too!

Dog On Oils

Chapter Four
Keep Calm, And Carry-On... Like A Porcupine!

4

Like a Porcupine! What? I'm not kidding. Check this out!

An ironically funny fact about me is that for most of my life, I've been naturally energetic. I'm excited about life and all that it holds every day of the week. My husband can attest! In the morning before my first cup of coffee, I am looking at the day and making my plan to seize it. What's so amusing about that little factoid? Well, to positively affect an aggressive, excited, or fearful dog you have to be confident and well ... CALM! Let me explain.

We recently rescued a small terrier, and it didn't take long to understand why she refused to stay put at her former home. She's on excitement overload incessantly bouncing around like she is on steroids. We affectionately call her, Ding Dong Peppercorn. If you think that is strange, please do not ask me the names of our other 12! Yes, thirteen dogs. It's a number we can't seem to get away from, no matter how much we have tried. And, believe me, we've tried! I will share later about what I affectionately call our *"barkers dozen."* So this sweet new addition is as full of energy as I am. I was amazed at how this pup brought our pack to life. And, she has helped me to see my energetic side as a beautiful thing.

Pay close attention here; I'm about to learn from a most unlikely source and teach you about something deeper involving excitement, confidence, and CALM.

One morning when my husband and I were sitting in a doctor's waiting room. My sweet UPS truck driving husband, who laughs loudly with me about how he daily goes from *"ups" to pups!* While in the waiting room watching a wildlife program on TV, I noticed a leopard stalking a porcupine. Heart racing, the cat was inches away from its prey, I looked away and told my husband I couldn't bear to see that kind of carnage so early in the morning! Gasp! Suddenly Ron said, *"Look, it's okay!"* When I glanced over, the leopard was limping away with one of the porcupine's quills protruding from its body. The porcupine was unfazed, sitting there effortlessly carrying on with his life. Completely CALM!

I want to always move forward in life like that porcupine calm and collected, knowing I am protected. Oh man, that rhymed! Yay me! Hands clapping! Wait! Here's the lesson;

Calm and collected means your dog won't be affected!

So learning how to be calm is key to helping your

dog settle down and not be affected by every external stimulus unfolding around him/her. Your emotions play a big part in stimulating your pet. They sense, they emulate, they respond to everything you are feeling. As I mentioned earlier, don't forget, essential oils can help your dogs during times of emotional overload. Well heck! Remember, they help you too! And, whether or not you have checked your own emotions, essential oils can be used as a tool to get both of you where you need to be. Can I reveal right now that certain essential oils calm you as soon as the aroma hits your limbic system? When you need to be calm, the blend Peace and Calming ® will quickly become one of your new BFFs. Lavender too has been used for millennia to bring a peaceful vibe over everything that has breath.

Then there's the fantastic blend Abundance™ that without fail, engages the nostrils of thirteen dogs when four can't stop eyeing and barking at seven tree trimming guys carrying enormous limbs down the side of our house by the french doors. As the dog's reactions escalated, I stood with my back to the doors and claimed that space, it worked for most of them quieting them right down. As for the rest, I pulled off the cap of my Abundance™ and waved the oil bottle in the air. Every nose engaged, shifting their attention, and the barking stopped. Here's a factoid to remember! Dogs can't use their eyes with intensity when their nose is full-on function. They are like a one-trick pony! It's downright amazing!

The Science of CALM

When my kiddos were younger, and their friends visited, we quickly recognized their buddies' level of CALM. If they displayed nervousness, our pack of pups, the *barkers dozen*, would go off like a flock of squawking seagulls. And I do not mean the eighties band! Every time one of their friends, Rey, walked in, he would nervously attempt to pet the little buggers, and in unison they would jump up some nipping at him. He and my son made several very creative attempts to overcome the barking and bad behavior. When they brought out the toy gun it was a bit disturbing. In the end, their adolescent boy brilliance and other semi-disturbing techniques proved slightly useful.

In my analytical playground of a mind, I started to ponder at length, a personal theory I call the Science of CALM. I wondered if I could genuinely be calm. Or, could I fake it? I began to think about what happens to our bodies when we are nervous or anxious. When we get crummy news or have to slam on the brakes to avoid an accident, these feelings arise in our bodies. I knew nervousness is felt in your torso area, specifically in your breastbone. Hmm, my cognitive wheels began to spin! If you can stabilize your breastbone, maybe you can trick your pet into thinking you are calm. Side note! Faking calm is a challenging thing to do if you are caught off guard.

But as I thought about it, I remembered the breathing exercises I learned from my Navy Seal BFF Beverly. Yes, she is a believer in breathing techniques too! She is so smart! Don't hate her. LOL! This breathing exercise is the one where you take air into your lungs and breathe it out through pursed lips in a prolonged and controlled way. And, boy oh boy, does it work! Talk about calm; it's like breathing out every bit of nervous! I'd also call it, anxiety-be-gone! When you intentionally breathe this way, every weight will lift right off you. This technique works wonders not only for you but for your pups also!

So, the next time Rey visited, I debriefed him in the front yard, teaching him the breathing technique and telling him that he needed to walk into our house with complete confidence. I shared that theoretically, every person is the boss of every dog. He didn't need to pet them to gain their approval. Through all of this, my analytical brain was in a tailspin, and I often wondered, "Am I out of my mind for thinking these things?" Within thirty seconds of entering our home all barking stopped, and there stood Reynaldo, *Prince of Puppy Politeness*, holding one of our pups with six others in a sweet circle around him.

Did Rey follow my instructions? Was I a genius? What really happened?

Well, in this case, Rey was the real genius because the next time he visited us, he walked in whistling one long-streaming note, and every one of our dogs responded with complete attention and silence. So, whether it was his whistle or confident body language that said, "I'm entering like I own the joint," from that day on, I affectionately called him my dog *"whistle-er."* Let me point out that his whistle was also like a melodic breathing technique that brought calm to the pack.

The very nature of calm and confident is that you have the power to let go of anything that is causing you anxiety and fear. If you check how you're feeling before you pull in to your driveway and let go of what is stressing you, you will notice a change in your body that will ultimately affect your pets. My daughter, Savannah, recently came to our home wearing the cutest dress and heels. She walked in, making a continual spewing sound then twirled around in what she called a *quieting flower circle*. I am not sure if this would work for all packs, but it did for ours! Instantly no barking!

Whatever your approach, confidence is vital. These are examples that I've seen work. Perhaps you can come up with your own. Do what works to bring calm to yourself and your dog. Then, you will be a genius too!

Dog On Oils

Chapter Five
The Barkers Dozen

5

So earlier I mentioned the thirteen dogs who call my house home. Thirteen, a number we can't seem to get away from no matter what. We've had more than that at times, but a steady thirteen seems to be our norm. Lord, help us! Our pets live anywhere from seventeen to twenty years, which helps explain why we have so many.

We have a *"less is more"* approach to being pet parents. We use wisdom, go easy on the traditional vet care, feed them well, including quite a bit of raw food. Early in our married life, our big dog Cowboy lived to be twenty eating cat food his entire life, even with our lack of real pet health knowledge. We vaccinated him minimally, and he survived a heartworm diagnosis. He was one tough doggie guy!

We've come a long way in so many things concerning our pets, kids, and grandchildren. Through it all, I will say this, you can't have an average of thirteen dogs for twelve years and not notice patterns of behavior.

I have a pretty awesome memory. Thank the good Lord above! It's scary and cool at the same time. I analyze pretty much everything nonstop all the time. You can't have that kind of a brain, a passion for peace and problem solving, and not use it for the greater good. So, while I know the science behind energy and the science behind essential oils, I am still amazed at their results and how implementing the positive use of one or the other, or both, can change a situation like night and day. And if a person will commit to implementing both regularly, they will witness some pretty amazing transformations.

By now, you know, I am a very excited person. Pretty funny when you think about the requirement of calm confidence as you handle your pet. Since learning about how our emotions affect our pets, I've become a master at reining in my excited energy for the sake of my dogs. And, let me tell you, the atmosphere of our home has completely turned around!

One year I took on a position with a design firm. Oh yeah, did I mention I am an artist and designer by trade? I have been a serial entrepreneur for nearly twenty-five years. But several years back, I decided to try a little experiment to see how it would be to work for someone else and ended up stressed to the core working an average of eighty hours or more on some weeks. What a ridiculous test! The result? A suppressed thyroid and Epstein Barr flare-up. Ugh! I will never know how I was physically and mentally able to work those hours. On top of it all, our house was flooded not once but twice! Can you imagine?

So when I got home every night, the first kisses and hugs didn't go to my sweet husband, all my energy and love was going to the loud and frenzied *Barkers Dozen*. The guilt I felt, the fatigue, then having to get up in the midnight hour to go back to work. I was a mess. The Barkers Dozen got all the *"baby Darlins"* I could give them as I talked to them like children with lots of love cuddling their insecurity and instability to the max.

The oppressive job was humiliating. I could work like a rockstar and still get scolded regularly. It was a sweet toxicity. I loved the clients and coworkers, but oh my word, the job was exhausting with little reward. It was not sustainable. When I was allowed to resign my position instead of being straight-up fired, it was bittersweet. Heavy on the bitter! And with all this super emotional junk I carried around, it was affecting my pups in the worst way.

> Yes, God can, will, and does use a dog to bring healing!

I further nurtured my insecurity as I tried to get over the job loss and feeling like I needed to make up for all the lost time at home. Shortly after going through this, I started following Cesar and took the training Beverly teaches on emotional release. Suddenly everything began to change, and, for the first time, I started seeing the evidence of it show up in the *Barkers Dozen*.

I began to look at everything in life from a different perspective. To say that God has used dogs to save my life might be an over-exaggeration, but it is one of many ways He has helped me. It all happened as I pursued balance by changing my thinking, which ultimately made way for health both in me and the *Barkers Dozen*. Yes, God can, will, and does use a dog to bring healing! Like He did for me through my formerly frenzied pack!

Dog On Oils

Chapter Six
A Life With No *Pulling*

6

It seems to me these days that around every turn, there is the idea that we are surrounded by stress. And, it appears around every corner there is a remedy. Headlines, social media, schedules, and work all push our priorities into a mega spin. But there is an uber-load of opportunities to find peace through gyms, exercise classes, and yoga studios of every type; regular yoga, hot yoga, and even goat yoga. What!?!? Each one is trying to kill us! LOL! I know! Anytime I try a new Pilates or yoga workout video, I joke with my husband that the instructor is trying to do me in. There are even meditation materials and apps to achieve what's called a *"zen state."* We can't forget the *"emotional support"* animals that people use to rid themselves of stress.

There are so many ways you can help your pet, and frankly, that your pet can help you. Sometimes *they* rescue you, and other times *you* save them. Like depression, I once heard that a way to overcome depression is to look around and find someone that needs help more than you. Your dog needs your help. He needs a stable pack leader. I am so thankful for service dogs that help people with emotional issues. I am also grateful for our veterans who have given so much for us. Isn't it great that support dogs are a tool and a gift for helping them get to a higher level of living life with emotional stability and health? Dogs don't just support people, but help restore their lives.

> Dogs don't just support people, but help restore their lives.

I recently took a trip out to a good friends' house in Santa Fe, New Mexico, and got to meet a more relaxed version of myself. And honestly, I got reacquainted with myself again! I wore sandals and dresses and put on makeup for the first time in like *forever*. I was ruined.

I drove their Jeep Rubicon for fourteen hours from Houston, Texas. After fishtailing through some treacherous terrain and struggling at times to keep the Jeep on the road, I was one tense girl upon arrival. But as soon as I stepped out of the vehicle onto the beautiful pathway of my destination that I now affectionately call *"heaven on Earth,"* every bit of my tension and anxiety instantly melted away. I fell in love with the gardens, house, the temperature. All of it! Except that Jeep! Whew, it gave me a run for my life on those roadways! Well I have to admit, even the jeep didn't look so bad after a good night's sleep. But I was officially ruined and trying to figure out how to shift my *"self"* to this new found heaven.

It was the most amazing escape from my hectic, though fun, life in Houston. No App or yoga studio could ever do this for me. Now when I need to relax, I get in my

Santa Fe *state of mind*.

One thing I also noticed in Santa Fe was my friend's dog's laid-back demeanor. Oliver, who we call *Ollie*, was cool as a cucumber. The Houston Oliver is a bit intense. I always tell my sweet friends that their dog's behavior is all their fault. Hahaha! Good friend, right? Smile! But there's no doubt that what I noticed in Santa Fe was the calm and laid-back version of Ollie. And guess what? I also witnessed a more relaxed version of his mama too.

One afternoon, we went to the neighborhood dog park, and I came upon an impromptu training session as a result of going to what I thought would be *"yappy hour."* To my surprise, about 98% of the dogs were calm. I thought, "This place is amazing!"

There are many ways to walk your dog off-leash, but this is a dream scenario, not a reality for most of us, especially city folks! I wanted to become famous for being the woman who could walk a pack of dogs with Dental Floss! I mean, the city doesn't specify the size of the leash. Right? But, if you put all the correct elements into action, you can have a peaceful, stress-free walk with *no pulling*.

A great idea at the end of your hectic workday is to take your pup out for a walk after you breathe in the relaxing aroma of Lavender essential oil. One idea I love to put in my clients' heads is that if the dog can stroll across the living room on his terms, even if he is active and needs exercise, he can by the same token walk calmly next to you as he saunters down the sidewalk for a walk.

It is all about how you start the exercise. First, establish complete calm before you put on the leash and go out the door, then you go out the door first. And if the dog wants to get ahead of you, walk your pet in a circle to position to dog behind you. And if your dog needs to calm down before the walk, don't worry, you are draining energy off your pup by making him wait. It is all exercise. As you allow calm to come, you are preparing the dog to walk with no pulling. And helping him to think the same thing you are thinking. Since a dog will never know how you got stressed or worried, get in the habit of directing your mind to positive thoughts. All these steps may seem impossible, but in time or no time at all, you will have success. Your ability to wait and follow through with this method is your greatest asset.

Some people don't like to walk their dog because of the pulling, And, they might be thinking they have to take their dog to months-long obedience training classes. No, you don't! When you put to practice the simple technique I shared above, you will have so much confidence and compliance from your dog that you will be training your neighborhood dog owners too.

Dog On Oils

Chapter Seven
Puppy Nose Best

7

Can I say, I love the nose of a dog? I do! I really do!

One of the most interesting aspects of a dog's nose is that it's the first of the senses developed in them as puppies, which will remain strong and vibrant through their senior years right up to the end of their life. Watching a senior dog who sleeps all day run like a puppy around the kitchen island at the smell of mealtime is a sight to see! I always make sure my pack is calm at feeding time, except for the elders. Their excitement is a pure celebration of their nose and an absolute joy.

A dog's nose saves lives by locating people and things, even disease, as they serve and protect. *"Sniffing for Safety,"* ought to be a slogan for these fantastic dogs. With 300 million receptor sites, a dog's nose is a powerful gift.

There is a term used to describe how pets react to specific maladies they suffer from time to time. "Zoopharmacognosy," also known as *animal self-medication*, because animals have been observed choosing certain natural elements for their healing. The best example of this is when you notice your pet eating grass. According to VetWest, dogs and cats choose certain grasses to ingest that help with dietary deficiencies, inducing vomiting, or elimination of intestinal parasites. It makes sense to me because God created every species on earth to know what to eat, how to forage, and how to help themselves maintain their health in the wild. Birds too! Even chickens seem to have a generational understanding about where to build their nests so that natural enemies cannot get to their eggs or their young.

Because *puppy nose best* acclimating your pet to essential oils is vital. When introduced as a young pup, the aromas of essential oils become normal to them. No matter the age, gently offering oils to a dog is both friendly and respectful. Forcing an essential oil on your dog when they are indicating they do not want to be exposed to it, can create a block in building trust. In my experience watching animals interact with essential oils, I have seen the theory of Zoopharmacognosy prove right.

Bubba, a big beautiful Rottweiler who lives in my neighborhood, needed some Tea Tree oil one day because of an ear infection. So I delivered a bottle to his family. As I handed the bottle to his mama, keys in hand with a dangling softball-sized pompom enticing Bubba, he reached up and grabbed what looked like a bouncing ball to him. Fun! And yes, I laughed, looking at this massive dog with rainbow fringe and fuzz protruding from his lips! When I reached down to get him to release the pompom, he refused, so I decided the Tea Tree oil could redirect his nose. Not only did the aroma redirect Bubba's nose, but he also spat out the fuzzy ball and started licking the top of the oil bottle with glee! His behavior confirms the Zoopharmacognosy theory that animals demonstrate this type of action as a sign. Bubba's licking was his way of saying, "Yes," to the oil. Wow! We applied Tea Tree to the ear, then visited over the next 30 minutes. Bubba's pet parents noticed he had not scratched his ear after applying the oil. Case closed! Amusingly and entertainingly, Bubba got the *medicine* he needed, and he chose it for himself!

Jasper, another sweetheart of a dog, all one-hundred fluffy pounds of him, the second time I showed up to give him a raindrop effleurage (a form of massage using feathering movements with the hands), he came right to me and laid down ready to receive. I'm telling you dogs love essential oils and sense by cognition that they are vital for their wellness.

Did I mention one of Beverly's pups is also named Jasper? Beverly gives Raindrops to many people in her home, so her massage room always has that unique aroma wafting through the air. Jasper and Beverly's other dog, Jasmine, along with their family cat gravitate to that room. Obviously, their nose is drawing them there! These pets were raised on oils!

If you are thinking, "*What is this Raindrop thing? I want to know more!*" No worries, I'm going to share more on it later. Just hang with me! One thing you NEED TO KNOW right now is that essential oils should NEVER be applied directly to a dog's nose. With all those receptors, it will throw them into sensory overload.

I've already mentioned a couple of blends that are super effective for engaging the noses of dogs, Abundance™ and Peace and Calming®. If you need to redirect your pets and change their current behavior patterns, remove the cap on one of these blends and wave the bottle around in the air to get their attention. It works!

Something else you need to know is that a dog's nose is hyper-engaged to food aromas, so let me share a bit about nutrition here as it relates to their sense of smell. Food is an incredible tool that can redirect and train your dog. Here's some "food for thought." Food is both nutrition and affection to a dog. Even if you never give your dog a treat, you still affect your dog day in and day out with food at mealtime.

> Food is both nutrition and affection to a dog.

Food provides energy for your dog. To that I say, regarding your dog's behavior, you have countless opportunities to use food to teach. One exercise that may not be new to everyone is that some breeds need to work for their food. Earning food can be as simple as making your pup give you eye contact and wait. Salivating is healthy for dogs. Waiting for food causes saliva production, which releases the digestive enzymes necessary for your dog's gastric health. Working for food can also be fun and challenging as you hide food in your yard.

In the case of Foxy and Minkie, two little ones I fostered until good friends of mine adopted them. These two overcame some pretty severe food aggression issues in a year. With patience and follow-through, it is not impossible even in older dogs like little Foxy and Minkie. In their case, we used food to rehabilitate them at every meal!

When taking care of dogs in overnight situations, initially many dogs do not want to eat their meal. So, I like to turn their meal into a challenge. Stella and Chewy's raw dehydrated dog food is one of my faves that can easily be given as treats. Wetting a bit of it, then giving a command turns the aversion to eating into a happy working for food situation. I love it, especially when we need to get going for the day, and all the dogs need to eat on schedule.

Research suggests that feeding your dog a nutrient-rich natural raw diet also improves behavior. Dogs are omnivores so they can eat fruit and vegetables in addition to meat! One of mine eats lettuce like it is a raw steak. I feed my *Barkers Dozen* raw grass-fed beef regularly. On infrequent, unavoidable occasions, I feed small amounts of high-grade kibble with no grain. The changes I saw in my pack after implementing a regular raw food regimen were remarkable and furthered their balanced behavior as I worked with them. It costs more, but I shop the sales, stock up, and freeze the food. When necessary, I feed them humanely sourced, corn-fed beef. It feels good to do this, which has value as I transfer that good feeling to my dogs as well. It brings a whole new meaning to the word

SATISFY!

So, when I think about the nose of a dog and why I love it so much. All that a dog's nose can do, it's no wonder I'm so thankful for it. A dog's nose is a cute little wet doorway into a dog's ability to learn and a way for us to bless them back by using their sense of smell to help them live a happy, healthy life!

Dog On Oils

Chapter Eight
Tips and Tricks to Help You Pass the Storm Drain

8

Focus & Conscious Thinking

While on a walk, look ahead to find something where you can focus, a tree, a car, or a hydrant. Walk toward it while you consciously think about going there. It will keep your attention on where you want to go, not on your dog. A storm drain will not be a problem as you practice. One of our dogs had an overwhelming amount of fear concerning the storm drains. As I dealt with her anxiety, I learned this focusing technique and began implementing it. I also realized this is a common occurrence in little dogs. Your focus will help you keep going when something else might derail the activity.

Apply the Science of CALM

If you are caught off guard, this can be a hard thing to do, but if you are not feeling calm, slowly breathe in and out through pursed lips. As you do, you will stabilize your sternum, and from what I have observed, it will significantly impact your dog. Or, if you are good at it, whistle, one continuous note if you can. Refer to page 29 for all the details about "The Science of CALM."

Out First In First

When going through any door or transition, be the first to go through. The same thing goes for the vehicle. Lead your pup into the car after he/she is calm. When possible, have them jump in on command; there are numerous benefits to their participation. Do the same routine when you arrive at your destination, which establishes in your dog a *"follower"* state of mind, like setting parameters for *"inside"* behavior.

On the Walk

Add a pep to your step with Peppermint oil. When you do not feel like a walk, take a whiff and let your dog get a smell too, it is both refreshing and energizing. Use it when you are in a hot climate, which I know well with this Houston heat. Add a drop of Peppermint to the back of your neck, and it will release the icy friend you need during a heatwave.

On a side note, if possible, put the phone away. Life these days leads a lot of us to believe we cannot be without our phones or technology, but wow the difference it can make without it and those noises it makes. One ding of the phone or a notification alert causes a reaction in your body. The sound signals stress, releasing the adrenaline hormone cortisol, which puts the body in a fight or flight mode. Your heart rate also goes up as a result. I don't want to sound like a clanging symbol here, but the reaction in your body triggers a response in your dog. I turned those notifications off for a year and watched the benefits unfold. Ding this, ding that, ding, ding, ding! The sounds condition you like a **Pavlovian dog!**

If you need to take your cell phone on the walk, I would recommend taking a bottle of Stress Away™ too. In fact, I always keep mine close by. I do not drink, and I limit carbs every chance I get, but I like to tell everyone that Stress Away™ blend smells like a margarita and a sugar cookie all rolled into one! It's like a long full exhale of "Ahhhhhh" in a bottle!

Yappy Hour at the Dog Park

Take your dog for a long walk before you enter the dog park. The best thing you can do for your dog is a walk demonstrating leadership to help him burn off excess energy. It's a great way to keep everyone safe from a fight. When you do, your dog will be calmed down by walking off his energy, so he will not be overwhelmed or try to go after another dog. And if he tends to be anxious, it will keep him safe from being a target for unbalanced dogs.

Claim it!

If your dog wants to take over the couch, the counter, the window, the door, or the guests, stop that behavior by simply going to the object or person claiming it or them for yourself. Send your dog back to his/her space. Follow-through is very important on this one. Consistency is the key to lasting change. Space equals respect. When the area belongs to you, claim it.

One More Thing on Follow Through

Make time to set up scenarios as opportunities for you to follow through. Remember, we are always teaching them something, and repetition helps them learn.

Fussy, Noisy Pups

When whining, fussing, protesting, instability, barking, or any unwanted behavior is unfolding, do not pet your dog. Even if he/she is a puppy. Be a mama dog, stay calm, and give a mama dog response, gently nudge and give a quiet Cesar "Cht!"

Nipping

Don't become your dog's object or chew toy. Always stay calm and move towards the pup with fluid motion, then give a mama dog response. Also, think about what kind of day you have had. Are you feeling hectic or anxious? Breathe. Sometimes they are nipping at stress. You can also redirect your pup with something to chew on if nipping is a teething issue.

Marking and Urinating in the House

It is always good to make sure your pet does not have a medical issue before addressing this as a behavior. One thing that I learned by trial and error was implementing an established consistent feeding schedule — making sure to feed canine appropriate nutrient-rich food. Mama dogs know when their pups need to go out. Monitor and keep them close by on a leash. If you can't keep them in a kennel, look for the signs and take them out when they signal the need to go. After feeding, sleeping, or playing, you may notice them circling, sniffing, or pacing. All are *"gotta go"* body language. Walk for leadership, thoroughly clean up accidents, and remain calm. If they are marking for territory, girl dogs do this as well as boys, all of the above techniques will be helpful. Also, see the magical *"silver concoction recipe"* below in TOOLS for clean up without a trace.

Tools for Cleanup without a Trace

Liquid colloidal silver is the BOMB for cleaning up your dog's accidents. Mix it up with one to two droppers between 30 -100 ppm of colloidal silver to a spray bottle of water using a dark glass bottle is best. Any other bottle will do, but effectiveness may wane with exposure to light. Spray area and in some cases, soak area with the solution. The urine molecules must come in contact with the silver. Not to be all super *"scientificky,"* but I learned this years ago and nearly got it on the market! Everything from stinky socks to stinky pets, one application, and the urine smells were eliminated. Well to deliberately be all *"scientificky,"* when the silver particle meets the microbe and permeates its cell wall, it stops cell replication, and that can stop a big bunch of stinky!

Dog On Oils

Chapter Nine
Essential Oils You Need Now and Why

9

Peppermint is refreshing and energizing.

Raven™ and **Eucalyptus** work wonders as bug repellents.

Valor® for courage! Put on your shoulders and breathe deeply; it's the oil of confidence!

DiGize™ and Peppermint for car sickness – apply to the pup's tummy before getting on the road.

Citrus Fresh™ and **Lemon**, "Odors away!"

Lavender for calm and sleeping through the night – there will be quite a bit of getting up in the middle of the night, depending on the age of your pet. But when you begin to see that your puppy can hold it for more extended periods, generally, they can go twice as long at night than in daytime hours. Use Lavender at bedtime. You can apply a bit of lavender to the hips or spine area for a full night's sleep.

Frankincense for focus and calming.

Stress Away™ can be used for calming and relaxation.

Thieves® and **Abundance**™ are great for capturing the attention of your dog's nose.

Panaway® can soothe aches and pains in us and our pups. It smells like **Aroma Seize**™, which is one of the raindrop oils.

Doggie Raindrop Technique

The Essential Oils: **Valor**®, **Oregano**, **Thyme**, **Basil**, **Wintergreen**, **Marjoram**, **Cypress**, **Peppermint**, **Ortho Ease**®, and **V-6**™

Acclimate your dog to the essential oil aromas before performing the first Raindrop on your pup. Do this by taking the cap off the bottle and slowly waving the bottle about 6 inches from the dog's nose. When your dog settles down, apply one drop to the palm of your hands, rub your hands together, then run your fingers through their fur repeating passes from the tail up the spine to top of their neck. You may make as many passes as you like for each oil, but a minimum of three is preferable. Repeat the process for each oil. **V-6 Carrier Oil** can be used to dilute each essential oil if desired and is preferred when a pup has been on medication or exposed to toxins. So, for first-time applications, carrier oil should be used as you introduce essential oils to your dog's body systems. Oils may be applied "neat," or undiluted, to your dog in future raindrops.

One or two drops at a time are enough.

Young Living's Animal Scents®

Infect Away™, **Mendwell™**, **ParaGize™**, and **PuriClean™** — my fave.

The **Animal Scents®** line supports your pet's wellness needs, and each blend is already diluted with a carrier oil. No mixing, no mess! Carrier oils slow down the absorption rate of essential oils in these blends, which are specially formulated with your pet in mind. All are soothing and gentle. As a bonus, a portion of all proceeds from the sale of Animal Scents goes to support Vital Ground Foundation, which is dedicated to protecting the habitat of grizzly bears. Bears need love too! And, I love how Young Living takes stewarding the earth and wildlife seriously! Supporting Vital Ground is their way of giving back!

Get Your Oils NOW

I would love for you to join me on a journey to a healthier, happier life! When you are ready to jump into the "oily lifestyle" (best decision ever), follow these simple steps:

Go to **youngliving.com**

- Chose "Become A Member"

My member number, 905835, should be pre-filled in the

sponsor and enroller ID sections. If it's not there, fill both sections with my number, and click CONTINUE.

- Choose your Premium Starter Kit!

If you want to, you can skip the Essential Rewards section for now and we can chat about that later!

- Continue enrollment.

- If you want to add more products to your order, do that here. Otherwise if you're good with your kit, click next.

- Fill out your info. (Be sure to write down your new member number, password, and pin number.)

- Then, purchase your kit!

About the Author

A self-described transformation junkie, Tracey has spent her life dedicated to changing the world around her and making it a better, more beautiful place for every living thing, whether in design, health, community outreach, or her philanthropic work. An animal lover from birth, she uses her gifts and talents to bring positive change to families and their homes through the joy and love God intended their dogs to give. Her wisdom and heart to teach and train has given her opportunities galore to see the remarkable results of bringing balance to the emotions of pets and their owners.

Website: www.dogonoils.com

Social Media

Facebook: Tracey L. Shreiber

Instagram @dogonoils @diffuserdog

YouTube: dogonoils

Praise for Tracey the Transformation Junkie

Cynthia Orta from Katy, TX

Jaxon, an African Rhodesian Ridgeback, stayed with us when our son got married two years ago. Due to his bad behavior while with us, I decided to get Jaxon some help.

I solicited Tracey Schreiber's services because I heard she was a dog whisperer. I feared that when Tracey met Jaxon, he would bite her, but she knew how to approach him, and to my surprise, she was able to control him and calm him down. I was in disbelief! Within five minutes, she set rules and boundaries for him. She took him on a walk, and I noticed he did not pull. She never looked him in the eye – almost ignoring him as she controlled him with hand gestures and few words. He obeyed her commands – sit, stop, no barking.

Tracey recommended a special rope leash that sits right behind Jaxon's ears, which allows us to control him. She suggested no more rewarding him with snacks! She trained Jaxon to obey without rewards. And it all worked! Tracey taught us how not to let him walk in front or lead the way when taking him for a walk and how to stop him from barking at passersby with hand gestures.

We don't share our food with Jaxon anymore. He is not allowed to act like the king of our home by sitting on the highest part of the couch or roaming around. Tracey taught us not to let him dart out the door as soon as we open it. Now we open the door widely and command him to 'stay' or 'wait,' and he does not take a single step until we say, "Go!"

The best part of Tracey's training method is that she is consistent and follows through with every command. Jaxon was turned around and is now a well-behaved dog!

My family and I are very grateful for her services. In the end, we learned that the problem was not Jaxon, but us.

Anna Doran from Houston, TX

When Tracey first arrived at our house to be a dog walker, I had no idea how helpful she would be to my family! The moment she walked into my house, she could immediately see how overwhelmed I was with our adorable puppy, Cooper, who was much too excited and energetic to listen. Tracey quickly picked up on my anxiety and calmed my nerves by telling me not to worry about Cooper at all. Tracey turned to Cooper and began calmly giving him instructions, taking control of the situation, and ensuring he minded her instructions. Throughout this first interaction, Tracey provided me with helpful tips and gave me instructions on how I should act around Cooper. She recommended a new collar, a prong collar, and even purchased one for our family to utilize on walks. My husband and I began practicing Tracey's tips around the house and immediately started seeing improvements in Cooper's behavior. Every walk became easier, Cooper was less distracted by external noises, and I began feeling in charge at my house again. I loved every minute!

The next week, a friend of mine arrived at our house for a four-week stay. The moment this new person entered our home, Cooper's behavior began to decline. With a new person in the home, he started following instructions less, and I felt like once again, I was losing control. Immediately, I reached out to Tracey, and she quickly came to our rescue. Tracey conducted training sessions with the new houseguest, and we even set up additional outside activities to help Cooper burn some energy and keep his mind focused. This assistance, as well as advice through multiple phone calls, helped ensure Cooper got back on the right path. During the most recent training session, Tracey participated in our daily household activities, such as making dinner, eating dinner, and putting food in the fridge to assess Cooper's behavior. Tracey evaluated Cooper and came up with a game plan to ensure Cooper minded throughout these activities. Now, whenever I make dinner and eat, Cooper happily stays in his area, and we have a relaxing evening!!

My favorite change yet in Cooper's behavior, is his

sleeping pattern. We were really struggling with getting Cooper to sleep easily and sleep through the night. Of course, we brought this complaint directly to Tracey, and she had an immediate solution, the use of lavender oil to calm Cooper down. The first night we used the lavender oil, Cooper fell asleep immediately and slept through the night! Since the introduction of lavender, Cooper has slept through the night every night, and therefore, we are sleeping through the night!! Every morning and every evening have been a blessing, thanks to Tracey, and we are really getting to enjoy our Cooper!

Gina Ortega of Springhill, FL

I met Tracey Schreiber on a flight from Houston to New York. We shared a row on the plane and became fast friends. She told me that she was driving a dog across the country to its new owner, and went on to say she was a dog behavioralist who had a lot of dogs herself. I told her I wanted to stuff my dogs and put them on a shelf. We laughed for a while about that comment! But, Tracey still asks how my dogs are doing. I'm sure she hopes she saved them from the shelf.

While she shared on that two-hour flight, I realized that my dogs were so bad because they were reacting to me. At first, I didn't believe her, and after that flight, I thought I would never hear from her again. She told me she would send me some calming oils and videos on how to command my dogs and get better behavior out of them.

We exchanged numbers, and low and behold a few days after getting home, she texted me to see how my dogs and I were doing. A day later, she sent me a video showing me how she commands her dogs and how it doesn't have to be stressful. I was amazed! I have two dogs and wanted to pull my hair out; she has thirteen! She showed me how my stress was coming out in my dogs' behavior. She taught me how to take control and to stay calm so they would react better. Well, I can report that my dogs are still at home and not on the shelf, and my life has become a lot less stressful.

Tracey is an amazing, caring, and very helpful person to everyone she meets. I'm now a proud new friend and a true believer in Tracey, and I think anything she does, she will put her all into it as she did for my dogs and me.

www.ingramcontent.com/pod-product-compliance
Lightning Source LLC
Chambersburg PA
CBHW052115070526
44584CB00017B/2488